BLASTER'S GUIDE
THIRD EDITION

Precision Blasting Services, Inc.
Post Office Box 189
Montville, Ohio 44064-0189, U.S.A.
Telephone: (440) 474-6700 - Fax: (440) 968-3967
URL: www.idc-pbs.com - Email: info@idc-pbs.com

Blaster's Guide

List of Tables and Charts

PRECISION BLASTING SERVICES PRODUCT AND SERVICE LIST

Training

Precision Blasting Services offers multiple courses to train people of all levels in the mining and explosives industry. Generally three day courses, on site in a special training facility. Covers all topics of blasting including:

>Rock Blasting and Overbreak Control
>Effective Quarry Blasting Methods
>Safety for Blasting and Explosive Use
>Underground Blasting Methods
>Blasting Geology
>and more!

Publications

Precision Blasting Services offers many other publications in the form of video, audio, and book. These publications relate to all different aspects of blasting and explosives.

BLASTER'S GUIDE
Third Edition

INTRODUCTION

This brief Blaster's Guide will provide methods to estimate burden, spacing, stemming and subdrilling as well as explosive loads.

Charts are available to help explain blast vibration and air overpressure. The new charts provide comparisons of blast vibration and normal environmental vibration as well as air overpressure compared to wind. These charts provide both the laymen and professional with an easy, understandable method to compare blast effects with normal activities and normal environmental phenomena.

The first section of the guide will provide a series of tables that, with little effort, can be used to determine average blast design dimensions.

The Blaster's Guide gives separate tables for estimating blast design dimensions in both USA.

Additional forms are also given for blasting plans, seismic monitoring reports and blasting logs etc.

This guide will enable the blaster to estimate dimensions in the field as well as provide the necessary forms for control of blasting operations.

QUICK REFERENCE CHARTS

BURDEN ESTIMATE CHART (Calculated with the Konya Burden Equation)

Assume that the blast is using a six inch diameter ANFO charge with a specific gravity of 0.8 and blasting in massive shale that has a specific gravity of 2.5. First, we calculate the ratio of the two densities by dividing 0.8 by 2.6. This equals 0.3. Both rock density and explosive density charts are enclosed.

Go to the "Burden Estimate" chart and find the approximate burden by using the density ration and charge diameter. For example, the burden would be 12.7 or about 13 feet.

BURDEN CORRECTED FOR GEOLOGIC STRUCTURE CHART

Once the burden is estimated under average conditions it can be further refined by considering geologic structure. This table offers some insight into the amount the burden will change with geologic structural considerations.

ROCK DENSITY CHART

This chart provides the rock density ranges for common rock types.

EXPLOSIVE DENSITY CHART

This chart provides the explosive density ranges for general explosive types

STEMMING AND SUBDRILLING ESTIMATE CHART

Once the burden is known go to the second chart, entitled "Stemming and Subdrill Estimate," to determine the approximate stemming and subdrilling needed. At a burden of 13 feet, the stemming distance would be 13 feet if drill cuttings are used. If drilling chips or crushed stone are used, the stemming depth would be 9.1 feet. Subdrilling would be approximately 3.9 feet.

HOLE SPACING ESTIMATE CHART

To determine the hole spacing along the row, first we have to decide whether the holes are firing on the same delay period or whether they are truly delayed one from another. We have to determine the L/B ratio by dividing the burden with the bench height. Assume that the bench height is 30 feet. To determine the spacing distance, take the 30 feet and divide it by the 13 foot burden which gives a L/B ratio of 2.3.

The "Hole Spacing Estimate" chart shows that for the L/B ratio of 2.25, we would have a multiplier of 1.42 times the burden if using the same delay time. Since the burden is 13 feet in the example, multiple 1.42 times 13 and obtain a spacing of approximately 18.4 feet. If the blastholes we delayed one from another, the multiplier is 1.16 times the burden or 15.08 feet.

TIMING ALONG ROWS

The delay time between holes in a row can be estimated using the chart for timing along rows. In the example used, we are blasting shale that would fall under the coal overburden column. The spacing for delay blasting was found to be 15 feet. The delay time to use would be 27 milliseconds.

DELAY BETWEEN ROWS

The delay between rows is critical if good results are desired. Delays can be estimated depending on the amount of piling or scattering desired. For our example with 6 inch diameter holes, we will assume we want a scattered pile. For a 13 foot burden this would require a delay of about 78 milliseconds.

STEMMING DECKS

When multiple decks of explosive are used in the blasthole, we want to select the stemming deck length so that propagation will not occur. The stemming deck chart can be helpful for this purpose. For example with 6 inch blastholes, the stemming between explosive decks in dry holes would be 3 feet, while in saturated holes it would be 6 feet.

LOADING DENSITY CHART

To determine the weight of explosive per foot of loaded hole use the "Loading Density" chart. Find the specific gravity of the explosive along the top of the chart. Values range from 0.8 to 1.6. Find the charge diameter along the left hand column.

Find the intersection of the proper specific gravity column and the horizontal line of the charge diameter. The answer is the loading density in pounds of explosive per foot of borehole. For the example with ANFO in 6 inch diameter charges, the load would be 9.81 lbs/ft.

KONYA'S BLAST EFFECTS SCALE

This chart breaks vibration into 20 different categories or scales. Blast effects and human perception levels are compared in this chart. The chart graphically shows activities which fall in the same vibration ranges.

KONYA'S ENVIRONMENTAL VIBRATION SCALE

This chart breaks vibration into 20 different categories or scales. Normal environment effects can easily be compared to blast effects and human perception with the same 20 scales used in the Blast Effects Chart. The chart graphically shows activities which fall in the same vibration ranges.

AIR OVERPRESSURE COMPARED TO WIND PRESSURE

The air overpressure resulting from blasting is compare in PSI and dB to wind equivalents in miles per hour.

RECORDKEEPING FORMS

BLASTING PLAN FORM

In addition to the tables, the Blaster's Guide contains forms that may be needed for reporting purposes by the blasting contractor. In specifications, one commonly requires a blasting plan. You may want to use the standardized "Blasting Plan" form as shown in the next section.

DRILL LOG FORM

When blasting in locations where one has many mud seams and mud pockets, one may request the contractor to keep a blasthole drill log. A copy of a "Blasthole Drill Log" is also included in this package of forms.

BLAST REPORT FORM

Commonly one requires the blaster to submit blast reports for every blast on the project. Standardized "Blast Report" forms are also included. Along with the blast report forms, there is an additional sheet called "Blasthole Loading Information." This is used when holes are loaded with tow or more types of explosive. This form can be used to record the hole number and the depth to which different explosives are loaded from the collar of the hole.

PREBLAST INSPECTION FORM

Before blasting begins on an operation, it is common to require a preblast survey to be conducted at the nearest homes. The Blaster's Guide includes "Preblast Survey" forms for both interior and exterior inspections.

SEISMIC MONITORING FORM

As blasting begins on the operation, one may want the contractor to report the results of his seismograph readings. Standardized "Vibration Report" forms are also included.

DRILL PATTERN INSPECTION FORM

In projects that are critical, blasting improperly can cause severe problems, the inspector may want to inspect both production blasting patterns and the presplit drillholes to determine the accuracy of drilling. The "Drill Pattern Inspection" form shows hole number and row number, and the inspector can measure the burden, spacing and depth for each hole.

PRESPLIT DRILLHOLE EVALUATION FORM

Often a tolerance is given for the drilling of presplit blastholes. If blastholes are not in the proper locations, one cannot expect good results. Two types of tolerances are commonly discussed. Tolerances at the collar of the holes and tolerance on the slope itself. For example, a special provision may indicate the blastholes must be drilled within 2 borehole diameters of their intended center. You can measure the spacing of the holes and indicate, by just checking yes or no, whether or not the spacing was within the tolerance.

In some specifications it is required that 95% of the holes be within a tolerance distance from one another and also in and out of the slope. This tolerance distance is commonly given as 6 inches. These same specifications may state that if more than 5% of the holes are outside the given tolerance, blastholes will be shortened to the depth at which the drilling tolerance is met. The "Presplit Drillhole Evaluation" form can be used after a blast to determine how many holes meet the desired tolerance and at what depth.

The blasting forms included in this Blaster's Guide can be photo copied for field use. For this reason no figure numbers are placed on these forms. These forms are also available to the contractor through commercial vendors.

TABLES

IN

U.S. UNITS

BURDEN ESTIMATE
(in feet)

CHARGE DIAMETER (inch)	DENSITY RATIO (DR) DENSITY OF EXPLOSIVE / DENSITY OF ROCK						
	0.2	0.3	0.4	0.5	0.6	0.7	0.8
1.25	2.3	2.6	2.9	3.1	3.3	3.5	3.7
1.50	2.8	3.2	3.5	3.8	4.0	4.2	4.4
1.75	3.2	3.7	4.1	4.4	4.6	4.9	5.1
2.00	3.7	4.2	4.6	5.0	5.3	5.6	5.8
2.25	4.1	4.7	5.2	5.6	6.0	6.3	6.6
2.50	4.6	5.3	5.8	6.3	6.6	7.0	7.3
2.75	5.1	5.8	6.4	6.9	7.3	7.7	8.0
3.00	5.5	6.3	7.0	7.5	8.0	8.4	8.8
3.25	6.0	6.9	7.5	8.1	8.6	9.1	9.5
3.50	6.4	7.4	8.1	8.8	9.3	9.8	10.2
3.75	6.9	7.9	8.7	9.4	10.0	10.5	11.0
4.00	7.4	8.4	9.3	10.0	10.6	11.2	11.7
4.25	7.8	9.0	9.9	10.6	11.3	11.9	12.4
4.50	8.3	9.5	10.4	11.3	12.0	12.6	13.2
4.75	8.8	10.0	11.0	11.9	12.6	13.3	13.9
5.00	9.2	10.5	11.6	12.5	13.3	14.0	14.6
5.25	9.7	11.1	12.2	13.1	13.9	14.7	15.4
5.50	10.1	11.6	12.8	13.8	14.6	15.4	16.1
5.75	10.6	12.1	13.3	14.4	15.3	16.1	16.8
6.00	11.1	12.7	13.9	15.0	15.9	16.8	17.5
6.25	11.5	13.2	14.5	15.6	16.6	17.5	18.3
6.50	12.0	13.7	15.1	16.3	17.3	18.2	19.0
6.75	12.4	14.2	15.7	16.9	17.9	18.9	19.7
7.00	12.9	14.8	16.2	17.5	18.6	19.6	20.5
8.00	14.7	16.9	18.6	20.0	21.3	22.4	23.4
9.00	16.6	19.0	20.9	22.5	23.9	25.2	26.3
10.00	18.4	21.1	23.2	25.0	26.6	28.0	29.2
11.00	20.3	23.2	25.5	27.5	29.2	30.8	32.2
12.00	22.1	25.3	27.9	30.0	31.9	33.6	35.1
13.00	23.9	27.4	30.2	32.5	34.5	36.4	38.0
14.00	25.8	29.5	32.5	35.0	37.2	39.2	40.9
15.00	27.6	31.6	34.8	37.5	39.9	42.0	43.9

INSTRUCTIONS FOR USE OF THE TABLE:
1. Divide density of explosive by density of rock to determine density ratio (DR).
2. Find density ratio in table, find charge diameter in column 1.
3. Find where both vertical column and horizontal row intersect and read burden in feet.

BURDEN CORRECTED FOR GEOLOGIC STRUCTURE
(in feet)

AVERAGE BURDEN	MASSIVE ROCK	BROKEN, JOINTED MANY WEAK LAYERS
3	2.9	3.9
4	3.8	5.2
5	4.8	6.5
6	5.7	7.8
7	6.7	9.1
8	7.6	10.4
9	8.6	11.7
10	9.5	13.0
11	10.5	14.3
12	11.4	15.6
13	12.4	16.9
14	13.3	18.2
15	14.3	19.5
16	15.2	20.8
17	16.2	22.1
18	17.1	23.4
19	18.1	24.7
20	19.0	26.0
21	20.0	27.3
22	20.9	28.6
23	21.9	29.9
24	22.8	31.2
25	23.8	32.5
26	24.7	33.8
27	25.7	35.1
28	26.6	36.4
29	27.6	37.7
30	28.5	39.0
31	29.5	40.3
32	30.4	41.6
33	31.4	42.9
34	32.3	44.2
35	33.3	45.5
36	34.2	46.8
37	35.2	48.1
38	36.1	49.4
39	37.1	50.7
40	38.0	52.0

ROCK DENSITY

ROCK TYPE	SPECIFIC GRAVITY	DENSITY (ton/yd^3)
Basalt	2.8 - 3.0	2.36 - 2.53
Diabase	2.6 - 3.0	2.19 - 2.53
Diorite	2.8 - 3.0	2.36 - 2.53
Dolomite	2.8 - 3.0	2.36 - 2.44
Gneiss	2.6 - 2.9	2.19 - 2.17
Granite	2.6 - 2.9	2.19 - 2.44
Hematite	4.5 - 5.3	3.79 - 4.47
Limestone	2.4 - 2.9	2.02 - 2.44
Marble	2.1 - 2.9	1.77 - 2.44
Micaschist	2.5 - 2.9	2.11 - 2.44
Quartzite	2.0 - 2.8	1.69 - 2.36
Sandstone	2.0 - 2.8	1.69 - 2.36
Shale	2.4 - 2.8	2.02 - 2.36
Slate	2.5 - 2.8	2.11 - 2.36
Trap Rock	2.6 - 3.0	2.19 - 2.53

EXPLOSIVE DENSITY

EXPLOSIVE TYPE	DENSITY (g/cm^3)
Granular dynamite	0.08 - 1.40
Gelatin dynamite	1.00 - 1.60
Cartridged slurry	1.10 - 1.30
Bulk slurry	1.10 - 1.60
Air-emplaced ANFO	0.80 - 1.00
Poured ANFO	0.80 - 0.85
Packaged ANFO	1.10 - 1.20
Heavy ANFO	1.10 - 1.40

STEMMING AND SUBDRILLING ESTIMATE
(in feet)

BURDEN	STEMMING (cuttings)	STEMMING (chips)	SUBDRILLING
3	3	2.1	0.9
4	4	2.8	1.2
5	5	3.5	1.5
6	6	4.2	1.8
7	7	4.9	2.1
8	8	5.6	2.4
9	9	6.3	2.7
10	10	7.0	3.0
11	11	7.7	3.3
12	12	8.4	3.6
13	13	9.1	3.9
14	14	9.8	4.2
15	15	10.5	4.5
16	16	11.2	4.8
17	17	11.9	5.1
18	18	12.6	5.4
19	19	13.3	5.7
20	20	14.0	6.0
21	21	14.7	6.3
22	22	15.4	6.6
23	23	16.1	6.9
24	24	16.8	7.2
25	25	17.5	7.5
26	26	18.2	7.8
27	27	18.9	8.1
28	28	19.6	8.4
29	29	20.3	8.7
30	30	21.0	9.0
31	31	21.7	9.3
32	32	22.4	9.6
33	33	23.1	9.9
34	34	23.8	10.2
35	35	24.5	10.5
36	36	25.2	10.8
37	37	25.9	11.1
38	38	26.6	11.4
39	39	27.3	11.7
40	40	28.0	12.0

INSTRUCTIONS FOR USE OF THE TABLE:
1. Find burden in column 1.
2. Determine if stemming is drill cuttings or rock chips.
3. Read across the row to determine appropriate stemming and subdrilling.

HOLE SPACING ESTIMATE

RATIO (L/B)	SAME PERIOD (F)	DELAY PERIOD (F)
1.00	1.00	1.00
1.25	1.08	1.03
1.50	1.17	1.06
1.75	1.25	1.09
2.00	1.33	1.13
2.25	1.42	1.17
2.50	1.50	1.18
2.75	1.58	1.22
3.00	1.67	1.25
3.25	1.75	1.28
3.50	1.86	1.31
3.75	1.92	1.35
4.00	2.00	1.40
>4.00	2.00	1.40

INSTRUCTIONS FOR USE OF THE TABLE:
1. Divide bench height (L) by burden (B) - (L/B = Ratio).
2. Find ratio in column 1 of table.
3. Determine if adjacent hole in row is firing on the same delay period or if it is delayed.
4. Go to appropriate column in table and obtain factor number (F).
5. Multiply factor number times burden (F x B = spacing in feet).

TIMING ALONG ROW
(in milliseconds)

SPACING (feet)	COAL OVERBURDEN	LIMESTONE, GRANITE, BASALT
3	5.4	4.5
4	7.2	6.0
5	9.0	7.5
6	10.8	09.0
7	12.6	10.5
8	14.4	12.0
9	16.2	13.5
10	18.0	15.0
11	19.8	16.5
12	21.6	18.0
13	23.4	19.5
14	25.2	21.0
15	27.0	22.5
16	28.8	24.0
17	30.6	25.5
18	32.4	27.0
19	34.2	28.5
20	36.0	30.0
21	37.8	31.5
22	39.6	33.0
23	41.4	34.5
24	43.2	36.0
25	45.0	37.5
26	46.8	39.0
27	48.6	40.5
28	50.4	42.0
29	52.2	43.5
30	54.0	45.0
31	55.8	46.5
32	57.6	48.0
33	59.4	49.5
34	61.2	51.0
35	63.0	52.5
36	64.8	54.0
37	66.6	55.5
38	68.4	57.0
39	70.2	58.5
40	72.0	60.0

DELAY BETWEEN ROWS
(milliseconds)

BURDEN (feet)	MINIMUM TIME	HIGH PILE	AVERAGE PILE	SCATTERED PILE	CASTING
3	6	9	12	18	24
4	8	12	16	24	32
5	10	15	20	30	40
6	12	18	24	36	48
7	14	21	28	42	56
8	16	24	32	48	64
9	18	27	36	54	72
10	20	30	40	60	80
11	22	33	44	66	88
12	24	36	48	72	96
13	26	39	52	78	104
14	28	42	56	84	112
15	30	45	60	90	120
16	32	48	64	96	128
17	34	51	68	102	136
18	36	54	72	108	144
19	38	57	76	114	152
20	40	60	80	120	160
21	42	63	84	126	168
22	44	66	88	132	176
23	46	69	92	138	184
24	48	72	96	144	192
25	50	75	100	150	200
26	52	78	104	156	208
27	54	81	108	162	216
28	56	84	112	168	224
29	58	87	116	174	232
30	60	90	120	180	240
31	62	93	124	186	248
32	64	96	128	192	256
33	66	99	132	198	264
34	68	102	136	204	272
35	70	105	140	210	280
36	72	108	144	216	288
37	74	111	148	222	296
38	76	114	152	228	304
39	78	117	156	234	312
40	80	120	160	240	320

STEMMING DECK

HOLE DIAMETER (inches)	DRY HOLES (feet)	WET HOLES (feet)
2	1.0	2.0
3	1.5	3.0
4	2.0	4.0
5	2.5	5.0
6	3.0	6.0
7	3.5	7.0
8	4.0	8.0
9	4.5	9.0
10	5.0	10.0
11	5.5	11.0
12	6.0	12.0
13	6.5	13.0
14	7.0	14.0
15	7.5	15.0
16	8.0	16.0

LOADING DENSITY
(in pounds per foot of borehole)

CHARGE DIAMETER (inch)	SPECIFIC GRAVITY (g/cm³)												
	0.80	0.90	1.00	1.10	1.15	1.20	1.25	1.30	1.35	1.40	1.45	1.50	1.60
1.00	0.27	0.31	0.34	0.37	0.39	0.41	0.43	0.44	0.46	0.48	0.49	0.51	0.54
1.25	0.43	0.48	0.53	0.59	0.61	0.64	0.67	0.69	0.72	0.74	0.77	0.80	0.85
1.50	0.61	0.69	0.77	0.84	0.88	0.92	0.96	1.00	1.03	1.07	1.11	1.15	1.23
1.75	0.83	0.94	1.04	1.15	1.20	1.25	1.30	1.36	1.41	1.46	1.51	1.56	1.67
2.00	1.09	1.23	1.36	1.50	1.57	1.63	1.70	1.77	1.84	1.91	1.97	2.04	2.18
2.50	1.70	1.92	2.13	2.34	2.45	2.55	2.66	2.77	2.87	2.98	3.09	3.19	3.41
3.00	2.45	2.76	3.06	3.37	3.52	3.68	3.83	3.98	4.14	4.29	4.44	4.60	4.90
3.50	3.34	3.75	4.17	4.59	4.80	5.01	5.21	5.42	5.63	5.84	6.05	6.26	6.67
4.00	4.36	4.90	5.45	5.99	6.27	6.54	6.81	7.08	7.35	7.63	7.90	8.17	8.72
4.50	5.52	6.21	6.90	7.58	7.93	8.27	8.62	8.96	9.31	9.65	10.00	10.34	11.03
5.00	6.81	7.66	8.51	9.36	9.79	10.22	10.64	11.07	11.49	11.92	12.34	12.77	13.62
5.50	8.24	9.27	10.30	11.33	11.85	12.36	12.88	13.39	13.91	14.42	14.94	15.45	16.48
6.00	9.81	11.03	12.26	13.48	14.10	14.71	15.32	15.94	16.55	17.16	17.77	18.39	19.61
6.50	11.51	12.95	14.39	15.82	16.54	17.26	17.98	18.70	19.42	20.14	20.86	21.58	23.02
7.00	13.35	15.02	16.68	18.35	19.19	20.02	20.86	21.69	22.52	23.36	24.19	25.03	26.70
7.50	15.32	17.24	19.15	21.07	22.03	22.98	23.94	24.90	25.86	26.81	27.77	28.73	30.65
8.00	17.43	19.61	21.79	23.97	25.06	26.15	27.24	28.33	29.42	30.51	31.60	32.69	34.87
8.50	19.68	22.14	24.60	27.06	28.29	29.52	30.75	31.98	33.21	34.44	35.67	36.90	39.36
9.00	22.06	24.82	27.58	30.34	31.72	33.10	34.48	35.85	37.23	38.61	39.99	41.37	44.13
9.50	24.58	27.66	30.73	33.80	35.34	36.88	38.41	39.95	41.49	43.02	44.56	46.10	49.17
10.00	27.24	30.65	34.05	37.46	39.16	40.86	42.56	44.27	45.97	47.67	49.37	51.08	54.48
10.50	30.03	33.79	37.54	41.29	43.17	45.05	46.93	48.80	50.68	52.56	54.43	56.31	60.06
11.00	32.96	37.08	41.20	45.32	47.38	49.44	51.50	53.56	55.62	57.68	59.74	61.80	65.92
11.50	36.02	40.53	45.03	49.53	51.79	54.04	56.29	58.54	60.79	63.04	65.30	67.55	72.05
12.00	39.23	44.13	49.03	53.94	56.39	58.84	61.29	63.74	66.19	68.64	71.10	73.55	78.45
13.00	46.04	51.79	57.54	63.30	66.18	69.05	71.93	74.81	77.69	80.56	83.44	86.32	92.07
14.00	53.39	60.06	66.74	73.41	76.75	80.09	83.42	86.76	90.10	93.43	96.77	100.1	106.7
15.00	61.29	68.95	76.61	84.27	88.10	91.94	95.77	99.60	103.4	107.2	111.0	114.9	122.5
16.00	69.73	78.45	87.17	95.88	100.2	104.6	108.9	113.3	117.6	122.0	126.3	130.7	139.4

INSTRUCTIONS FOR USE OF THE TABLE:
1. Select the proper specific gravity of the explosive (range 0.8-1.6).
2. Select explosive diameter from the first column.
3. Find the intersection of specific gravity column and charge diameter row and read loading density in pounds/foot

Air Overpressure Compared to Wind Pressure

Wind Equivalent	Standards		
mph	dB	psi	
329.09	180	3	Structural Damage
268.70	176	2	Plaster Cracks
134.35	164	0.5	Windows Break
104.07	160	0.3	
32.91	140	0.03	OSHA Max. 100 Impacts/Day
15.90	128	0.007	US Bureau Of Mines Max.
10.41	120	0.003	OSHA Max. 10,000 Impacts/Day
3.29	100	3×10^{-4}	Pneumatic Hammer
1.04	80	3×10^{-5}	
0.33	60	3×10^{-6}	Conversational Speech
0.10	40	3×10^{-7}	
0.03	20	3×10^{-8}	
0.01	0	3×10^{-9}	Threshold Of Hearing

RECORDKEEPING

FORMS

BLASTING PLAN

Form provided by Precision Blasting Services

Location: _____ Job: _____ Date: _____

Type of Shot: _____ Station: _____

Type of Material: _____

Distance to Nearest Structure: _____ feet

Production Blast:

Number of Holes: _____ Hole Diameter: _____ Drill Angle: _____

Burden: _____ feet Spacing: _____ feet Depth _____ feet

Stemming: _____ feet Stemming Material: _____

Subdrilling: _____ Lift Height: _____

Method of Firing: (check one) Electric: _____ Non-Electric: _____

Sequential Timer: (check one) Yes: _____ No: _____ Timer Setting(s): _____

Surface Delay Periods: _____

Downhole Delay Periods: _____

Types of Explosives: _____

Size of Primers: _____

Primer Locations: _____

Trade Names of Explosives: _____ Amount: _____

_____ Amount: _____

_____ Amount: _____

_____ Amount: _____

Trade Names of Primers: _____ Amount: _____

_____ Amount: _____

_____ Amount: _____

Trade Names of Initiators: _____ Amount: _____

_____ Amount: _____

_____ Amount: _____

Maximum Lbs/Delay: _____

Anticipated Vibration Level: _____

Scaled Distance: _____

Air blast Scaled Distance: _____

Anticipated Air Blast Level: _____

NOTE:
1. Provide drawing of pattern, initiator hookup, hole firing times and cross section of blasthole showing explosive loads and primer locations, depth, subdrill, stemming, etc.
2. Include manufacturer's data sheets for all products.

BLASTING PLAN (continued)

Form provided by Precision Blasting Services

Controlled Blast:

Check One: Presplit: _____   Cushion Blast: _____   Line Drill: _____

Diameter of Drillhole: Hole Depth: _____

Drillhole Angle: _____

Method of Initiation: _____

Delays Used: _____   Holes/Delay: _____

Describe Methods Used To Maintain Hole Alignment:

_____

_____

_____

Buffer Row: Hole Diameter: _____   Charge Diameter: _____

             Total Charge: _____   Burden: _____

             Spacing: _____   Depth: _____

Trade Names of Explosives: _____   Amount: _____

                              _____   Amount: _____

                              _____   Amount: _____

                              _____   Amount: _____

Trade Names of Primers: _____   Amount: _____

                              _____   Amount: _____

                              _____   Amount: _____

Trade Names of Initiators: _____   Amount: _____

                              _____   Amount: _____

                              _____   Amount: _____

NOTE:
1. Provide drawing of pattern, initiator hookup, hole firing times and cross section of blasthole showing explosive loads and primer locations, depth, subdrill, stemming, etc.
2. Include manufacturer's data sheets for all products.

BLASTHOLE DRILL LOG

Form provided by Precision Blasting Services

DATE: _____   JOB/SHOT: _____   STATION: _____

BURDEN: _____ FT.   SPACING: _____ FT.   HOLE DIAMETER: _____IN.

NOTE: ALWAYS NUMBER HOLES LEFT TO RIGHT ALONG ROW FROM BEHIND SHOT LOOKING
       TOWARD FACE.

HOLE NO.	ROW NO.	INDICATE SEAMS/MUD/SOFT LAYERS

BLASTHOLE DRILL LOG (continued)

Form provided by Precision Blasting Services

DATE: _____   JOB/SHOT: _____   STATION: _____

BURDEN: _____ FT.   SPACING: _____ FT.   HOLE DIAMETER: _____ IN.

NOTE: ALWAYS NUMBER HOLES LEFT TO RIGHT ALONG ROW FROM BEHIND SHOT LOOKING
       TOWARD FACE.

HOLE NO.	ROW NO.	INDICATE SEAMS/MUD/SOFT LAYERS

BLASTING REPORT

Form provided by Precision Blasting Services

Location:	Report No.:	Date:

	Charge / Hole Number	Depth (ft)	Stemming (ft)	Total Charge Weight / Delay (Lbs)

Type of Shot: _____   Exact Time: _____

Station Number: _____

Type of Material: _____   Shot Grid: _____

Type of Blast: _____

(To nearest occupied building neither owned or leased)

#1 Seis. Locat.: _____   Dist to Seis.: _____ (ft) Grid: _____

#2 Seis. Locat.: _____   Dist to Seis.: _____ (ft) Grid: _____

Number of Holes: _____   Stemming (ft): _____

Diameter (mm): _____   Type of Stemming: _____

Hole Depth (ft): _____   Face Height (ft): _____

Delay Periods: _____

Spacing (ft): _____   Subdrilling (ft): _____

Burden (ft): _____   Number of Rows: _____

Method of Firing: _____

Type of Circuit: ☐ Series ☐ Parallel

Maximum Charge Weight / Delay: _____ Lbs / delay

Temperature: _____ °F

Weather: ☐ Clear   ☐ Cloudy   ☐ Rain   ☐ Snow

Wind From: ☐ N   ☐ NE   ☐ E   ☐ SE

☐ S   ☐ SW   ☐ W   ☐ NW

Fragmentation: ☐ Excellent ☐ V. Good ☐ Good ☐ Fair ☐ Poor

Backbreak: ☐ 3m   ☐ 6 ft   ☐ 9 ft   ☐ 12 ft   ☐ 15 ft or more

Trade Name of Explosive	Amount (Lbs)
Total:	

Powder Factor: _____ Lbs/yd³	Total Weight (Lbs):
Remarks:	Material Produced (yd³):
	Superintendent Sig.:
	Blaster's Signature:
	License or S.S. No.:

BLASTING REPORT (continued)

Form provided by Precision Blasting Services

Charge / Hole Number	Depth (ft)	Stemming (ft)	Total Charge Weight / Delay (Lbs)	SHOW DIMENSIONS ON SECTIONS, INCLUDE DEPTH OF POWDER
				PRIMER(S) LOCATION
				SKETCH PATTERN, SHOW INITIATION HOOK-UP

BLASTING REPORT

Form provided by Precision Blasting Services

Location:	Report No.:	Date:

	Charge / Hole Number	Depth (m)	Stemming (m)	Total Charge Weight / Delay (Kg)

Type of Shot: _____ Exact Time: _____

Station Number: _____

Type of Material: _____ Shot Grid: _____

Type of Blast: _____

(To nearest occupied building neither owned or leased)

#1 Seis. Locat.: _____ Dist to Seis.: _____ (m) Grid: _____

#2 Seis. Locat.: _____ Dist to Seis.: _____ (m) Grid: _____

Number of Holes: _____ Stemming (m): _____

Diameter (mm): _____ Type of Stemming: _____

Hole Depth (m): _____ Face Height (m): _____

Delay Periods: _____

Spacing (m): _____ Subdrilling (m): _____

Burden (m): _____ Number of Rows: _____

Method of Firing: _____

Type of Circuit: ☐ Series ☐ Parallel

Maximum Charge Weight / Delay: _____ Kg / delay

Temperature: _____ °C

Weather: ☐ Clear ☐ Cloudy ☐ Rain ☐ Snow

Wind From: ☐ N ☐ NE ☐ E ☐ SE

☐ S ☐ SW ☐ W ☐ NW

Fragmentation: ☐ Excellent ☐ V. Good ☐ Good ☐ Fair ☐ Poor

Backbreak: ☐ 3m ☐ 6 m ☐ 9 m ☐ 12 m ☐ 15 m or more

Trade Name of Explosive	Amount (Kg)
Total:	

Powder Factor: _____ Kg/m³

Remarks:

Total Weight (Kg):	
Material Produced (m³):	
Superintendent Sig.:	
Blaster's Signature:	
License or S.S. No.:	

BLASTING REPORT (continued)

Form provided by Precision Blasting Services

Charge / Hole Number	Depth (m)	Stemming (m)	Total Charge Weight / Delay (Kg)

SHOW DIMENSIONS ON SECTIONS, INCLUDE DEPTH OF POWDER

PRIMER(S) LOCATION

SKETCH PATTERN, SHOW INITIATION HOOK-UP

BLASTHOLE LOADING INFORMATION

Form provided by Precision Blasting Services

EXPLOSIVE LOADING DENSITY HOLE / CHARGE NUMBER	TO:	TO:	TO:	TO:	EXPLOSIVE LOADING DENSITY HOLE / CHARGE NUMBER	TO:	TO:	TO:	TO:
1					31				
2					32				
3					33				
4					34				
5					35				
6					36				
7					37				
8					38				
9					39				
10					40				
11					41				
12					42				
13					43				
14					44				
15					45				
16					46				
17					47				
18					48				
19					49				
20					50				
21					51				
22					52				
23					53				
24					54				
25					55				
26					56				
27					57				
28					58				
29					59				
30					60				

VIBRATION REPORT

Form provided by Precision Blasting Services

EVENT:_____ SHOT:_____ SEISMOGRAPH LOCATION:_____

LOCATION:_____ DATE:_____ TIME:_____

STATION:_____

SHOT POSITION: COORDINATES: EAST:_____ FT   NORTH:_____ FT

STATION:_____

SHOT POSITION: COORDINATES: EAST:_____ FT   NORTH:_____ FT

DISTANCE FROM SHOT:_____FT

MAXIMUM CHARGE WEIGHT PER DELAY:_____LBS

AIR OVERPRESSURE:_____Db

	RADIAL	TRANSVERSE	VERTICAL	VECTOR SUM	MAXIMUM
PPV					
FREQUENCY					

JOB_____   INSPECTOR/BLASTER_____

PREBLAST SURVEY

Form provided by Precision Blasting Services

EXTERIOR REPORT

Property Owner: _____ | Page ____ of ____ Pages

Outside Photos Taken: Yes _____   No _____   B&W _____   Color _____

Description of Lot: Level _____   Sloping to front _____   Sloping to rear _____   Or to Side _____

Standing Water or Pooling Area: Front _____ Back _____ Left _____ Back _____

Condition Codes: (E) - Excellent (G) - Good, not New (F) - Fair

Remarks

Roofs		Type of Material	
Siding	_____	Type of Material	_____
Gutters/Spouts	_____	Type of Material	_____
Driveway	_____	Type of Material	_____
Foundation	_____	Type of Material	_____
Walkway(s)	_____	Type of Material	_____

Porch(es) _____   Patio(s) _____   Windows _____

Chimney(s): Brick _____   Stone _____   C-Block _____   Metal _____

Front (facing foundations)   Right   Left   Rear

Detached Buidlings: Number: Condition:

Garage(s) _____

Barn(s) _____

Shed(s) _____

Utility Building(s) _____

Other(s) _____

PREBLAST SURVEY

Form provided by Precision Blasting Services

INTERIOR REPORT

Property Owner: _____ | Page _____ of _____ Pages

Room: _____ Entered From: _____

Walls:	Plaster ___	Dry Wall ___	Panel ___	Paper ___	C. Block ___	Other ___
Ceiling	Plaster ___	Dry Wall ___	Ac. Tile/Panel ___	Paper ___	Open C. ___	Other ___
Floor	Carpet ___	Linoleum ___	Square Tile ___	Wood ___	Concrete ___	Other ___

Wall   Ceiling/Floor

Remarks: _____
_____

Room: _____ Entered From: _____

Walls:	Plaster ___	Dry Wall ___	Panel ___	Paper ___	C. Block ___	Other ___
Ceiling	Plaster ___	Dry Wall ___	Ac. Tile/Panel ___	Paper ___	Open C. ___	Other ___
Floor	Carpet ___	Linoleum ___	Square Tile ___	Wood ___	Concrete ___	Other ___

Wall   Ceiling/Floor

Remarks: _____
_____

DRILL PATTERN INSPECTION FORM

Form provided by Precision Blasting Services

DATE: _____ STATION: _____

SHOT/JOB: _____ INSPECTOR: _____

HOLE NUMBER	ROW NUMBER	BURDEN (feet)	SPACING ____ inches ____ feet	DEPTH (feet)

PRESPLIT DRILLHOLE EVALUATION FORM

Form Provided by Precision Blasting Services

Date: _____ Job/Shot: _____ Station: _____ Inspector: _____

Drill Angle: _____ Spacing Tolerance: _____ Angle Tolerance: _____

Hole Number	Spacing (Hole Collar)	Spacing Tolerance		Hole Depth to Drill Angle Tolerance	Angle Tolerance	
		Yes	No		Yes	No

PRECISION BLASTING SERVICES

PRODUCT

&

SERVICE

LIST

PRECISION BLASTING SERVICES
PRODUCT AND SERVICE LIST
Prices as of 1-8-11

CONSULTING

Our services include blast design optimization for increased productivity, vibration monitoring and control, research and testing, litigation support, blasting complaint investigation, computer aided blasting error/accident analysis, and blasting safety and accident prevention.

Please call our office for additional information or scheduling.

TRAINING

Precision Blasting offers seminars for managers and supervisory personnel, blaster training, and field courses for "Hands On" experience. Seminars are taught by Calvin J. Konya, who received his Ph.D. in Mining Engineering from the University of Missouri at Rolla and other highly experienced instructors. Dr. Konya was a professor at Ohio State University doing blasting research and teaching in explosives and blasting, and has over three decades in worldwide field experience.

The training will be conducted at the Academy for Blasting and Explosives Technology in Northeast Ohio or at the Clients desired location.

Please call our office for information on future seminars or to schedule an in-house seminar.

ROCK BLASTING AND OVERBREAK CONTROL - This seminar is a guide to efficient blast design and vibration control for heavy construction, mining and quarrying projects. The fourth edition of the former Federal Highways Administrations "Rock Blasting and Overbreak Control" is the text used for this seminar.   This seminar provides current technology on blasting, vibration control, and new revised blasting specifications for surface blast design projects. Rock Blasting and Overbreak Control seminar is a must for contractors, DOT, FHWA, USACE, USBR or anyone in the blasting industry interested in practical, effective methods and procedures.

EFFECTIVE QUARRY BLASTING METHODS - Does your company do its own blasting or do you rely totally on shot service from another company? Ask yourself if the quarry has any of the following concerns: Does the breakage or sizing need improvement? Are the quarry walls torn up? Is the quarry floor level? Are costs too high? Are blast vibrations disturbing the neighbors? If the answer is yes to any of the above questions then join us for this seminar.

SAFETY FOR BLASTING AND EXPLOSIVES USE - The seminar will teach participants how to safely work with explosives. The seminar coves the use of explosives, initiators, primers and prevention of premature explosions. The seminar will discuss proper safe blasthole loading methods. Methods and causes of flyrock, vibration damage and airblast damage will also be reviewed. The topics will be illustrated with actual case histories given. This seminar is a "must attend" for all DOT, FHWA, BLM, construction contractor and quarry and mining personnel responsible for the blast design and wall on blasting projects. Instructor is Mickey Bradley.

NEW!!! SURFACE BLAST DESIGN WORKSHOP - This is the seminar requested by professionals who want to update their design and problem solving skills. The seminar is for those who have already taken either the Quarry Blasting or Rock Blasting and Overbreak Control seminar and desire more knowledge and practice in problem solving and calculations for advanced blast design.

NEW!!! BLASTING GEOLOGY - In order to effectively blast in a safe and productive manor, the blaster must understand the local geology and rock types as well as the interaction of geology and blast design. The joints, bedding planes, sheeting, voids, weathering etc. can require changes in design to function properly. The geologic reports, RQD, percent recovery all give blasters important information for estimating costs and designing blasts

OTHER SEMINARS AVAILABLE - Some past seminars have been taught on subjects such as Blasting Concrete, Blasting for the Chemical Lime Industry, Blasting in Open Pit Mines, Introduction to Blasting, Underground Blasting, Underwater Blasting, Vibration And Airblast Control, and Writing Effective Specifications for Construction Projects
These seminars can be of any duration. Some clients need a two- day seminar to get PDU continuing education credits for professional engineering licenses or for blasting license renewal. We tailor a seminar to meet your needs.

SEMINARS AT YOUR FACILITY - We have taught Seminars at Clients facilities in the USA and also in many foreign countries. We can work with you to tailor a seminar to meet your needs.

BLASTING SOFTWARE WE CAN RUN FOR YOU
(Get A Second Opinion for a Low Cost)

BLAST DESIGNER
One can quickly determine burdens, spacing, stemming, sub-drilling, powder loads and many other important design variables for estimating blasting jobs and for the design of patterns. New design formulas or traditional powder factor calculations can be used for design. Powder factors, total drill footage and other important information is available in a matter of seconds. The program allows for on-screen comparison of four different designs.

BLASTING COST ANALYST
One can quickly compare costs, calculate the cost per cubic yard (cubic meter) and the cost per ton resulting from up to four different blasting patterns. One can change burden, spacing, hole depth, stemming, sub-drilling, hole diameter, priming and initiators to determine the effects on the cost. One can also consider the effects of up to three different explosives in each hole, initiators, primers, boosters, drilling cost, liners, pumping, shot services and seismic monitoring on the total cost picture. One can compare the cost per energy unit to select the most efficient cost effective explosives for the particular job.

BREAKER
This program can predict and compare relative difference in fragmentation between blasts. It can compare the changes in fragmentation due to many normal blasting variables, such as burden, spacing, bench height and the type of explosive used. The program will also work with two different explosives in the borehole. A scientific method to determine the effects of rock strength and geologic structure is also

provided. The program will print the percentage, weight and volume of material produced in various size ranges and display graphic interpretations in the form of line and bar graphs.

CHEF - CALCULATIONS FOR HIGH EXPLOSIVE FORMULATIONS

Many small companies mix ingredients to provide the user with emulsions, water gel, and heavy ANFO types of explosives. This software provides thermodynamic calculations, to easily determine optimum mixtures of ingredients, and calculates the oxygen balance for explosive mixtures, detonation velocity, temperatures and pressures for Detonation State and Explosion State. It also has the ability to calculate the temperature and pressure which result from decoupled charges. This is the Expansion State and it provides useful information when charge volumes are smaller than borehole volumes or charge diameters are smaller than borehole diameters.

CONTROLLED BLASTING

The Controlled Blasting program considers pre-splitting, trim (cushion) blasting and line drilling methods for wall control. For mining applications, the Air Deck Method can also be used. The program uses basic information and current design formulas to determine powder loads, bottom loads, stemming distances, and spacing for different methods of controlled blasting.

DELAY SELECTOR

The Delay Selector software is a unique program that enables the operator to select the proper millisecond delay time to accomplish specific effects in blasting. Delay times are dependent on many factors, a few of which are rock type, rock structure, burden, spacing and the overall effects one wants to achieve. There is no simple general solution if one wants to optimize production. The delay times are calculated from hole to hole along a row and between rows. By selection of the proper delay time, one can enhance wall control, reduce flyrock, increase fragmentation and decrease vibration. Many other parameters can also be controlled by proper timing. The Delay Selector program allows the user to prioritize the most important blast effects and select delay times based on the blast performance he needs. The Delay Selector program can be used in conjunction with Blast Designer and Pattern Designer to fully evaluate or design efficient blasts.

DRILLING COST ANALYST

Drilling Cost Analyst is a program that allows the user to compare fixed and/or variable costs of all types of blasthole drills. The program considers labor, daily maintenance, bit, steel, pipe, patterns and power costs. The costs are identified per hour, per foot or cubic yard (per meter or cubic meter).

PATTERN DESIGNER - Non-Electric, Electric & Universal Initiation Systems

Pattern Designer calculates firing times and checks blasting patterns for SURFACE AND UNDERGROUND ROUNDS and for square or staggered patterns. Versions are available for electric initiation and non-electric initiation. The universal version handles both electric and non-electric. No other software has our quick-to-load pattern libraries or build-your-own pattern capabilities. The programs can work with up to 40 holes per row, 10 rows and 10 decks per hole. Patterns can be irregularly shaped, with lost holes anywhere in patterns. The software allows the user to quickly find timing overlaps of any number of holes and determine the PROBABILITY of such overlaps. The program also shows animated firing of the patterns and decks. A pattern design report can be produced. One can design an infinite number of patterns quickly and easily. These patterns can be saved for future convenience. Many pattern libraries are available for fast and easy pattern design and analysis.

SHAFT DESIGNER

SHAFT is an efficient tool to quickly design shaft blasting jobs. Shafts, vertical or inclined, are used to provide access from the surface to underground entries or from one level to another in a mining operation.

STRUCTURAL BLAST DESIGNER

Structural Blast Designer is a unique program developed in Europe by individuals with decades of experience in building and structural demolition. The program designs blasting patterns and powder loads for 45 different structural elements. The elements can be brick, concrete and reinforced concrete. The software provides designs for demolition of columns, piers, slabs, arches, chimneys and various other structural members. The program designs powder loads, number of decks, burden, spacing and hole layout for each structural element.

VIBRATION ASSISTANT

This program does everything described below for Vibration Consultant; and offers other unique features. It helps the user determine if the vibration is at normal expected levels or if levels are much higher than anticipated. The program automatically puts an asterisk next to the data to show the user it is time to re-evaluate the blasting procedure. The user then has the choice to either use this data in further analysis, or to disregard the data from the analysis. The data will remain within the data file, but will not be used for calculation since it is an abnormality and not something that is normally occurring. If both the blast and monitoring coordinates are considered, the program automatically calculates the distance from the blast as well as the azimuth from the blast to the seismograph. This helps to maintain accurate distances between monitoring points, and to exactly locate monitoring points for future reference. The program allows the use of data from all three components; vertical, radial, transverse as well as peak vector sum. One can run an analysis using the data from any of these three components, the vector sum, or the program can automatically select the maximum vibration level from any of the three components.

VIBRATION CONSULTANT

This program performs a linear regression of blast vibration data and will predict peak particle velocity at any distance from the blast. The software will produce a table showing the maximum charge-per-delay for various distances to achieve a specified maximum vibration level. One has the choice of printing graphs of peak particle velocity versus scaled distance, peak particle velocity versus frequency and charge weight per delay versus distance. The program also performs a linear regression analysis of air overpressure and plots air overpressure versus scaled distance. The program will predict overpressure values at any distance from the blast.

ALL PROGRAMS ARE NOW AVAILABLE FOR "PBS" TO RUN FOR YOU

BLASTING PUBLICATIONS

Rock Blasting and Overbreak Control
Written by Dr. Calvin J. Konya and Dr. Edward J. Walter. The text includes blast design, pattern design, overbreak control, site conditions and field procedures, applications, vibration and seismic waves, an inspector's guide, and much more.

The Blaster's Guide
The Blaster's Guide will provide methods to estimate burden, spacing, stemming and subdrilling as well as explosive loads. The first section of the guide will provide a series of tables that, with little effort, can be used to determine average blast design dimensions. Additional forms are also given for blasting plans, seismic monitoring reports and blasting logs. The guide will enable the blaster to estimate dimensions in the field as well as provide the necessary forms for control of blasting operations.

Blast Design
Precision Blast Services is proud to announce it's newest publication for the blasting industry. Blast Design covers the design of both surface and underground blasts. Blast Design is a must for anyone in the blasting industry. It was written by Dr. Calvin J. Konya. This book is written for the professional blaster or explosive engineer. This book is written in Metric Units (SI).

Proper Utilization of Explosive Energy
- A 2-Hour Comprehensive Introduction to the Science of Explosives

This training video is presented by Dr. Calvin J. Konya. Dr. Konya is the founder and president of Precision Blasting Services and received his Ph.D. in Mining Engineering from the University of Missouri at Rolla. The video is available in VHS format for NTSC (North American), PAL or SECAM system.

The video covers the sources of the two distinct types of explosives energy, the manner in which the maximum energy is released, methods to identify problem explosive mixtures, the manner in which the shock and explosives energy breaks rock, the different blasting parameters and their effects on the mechanics of breakage, the effects of geological features on breakage, and the method in which fracturing occurs.

SHIPPING & HANDLING
Prices include free shipping within the USA.

EMULSION PLANTS

Emulsion Plants
Emulsion Explosives Equipment, a division of Precision Blasting Services, offers the design and manufacturing of emulsion plants. These state of the art plants are custom built to meet the needs of the individual client. Can make packaged, bulk, and hardened emulsions. These plants can produce in any climate. Portable plants are also for sale which can easily be moved by truck, train, or ship.

Contact us for more info at info@idc-pbs.com

OTHER PRODUCTS

- Blasting Workstation - notebook computer with various computer programs pre-loaded

- Dewatering Pumps

- Seismographs

- Blasting Machines

- Emulsion Technology

- Blasting Mats

- Emulsion Pumps

- Remote Blasting Machines

----
cut along dotted line

Please send me additional information on the following products and/or services:

- ☐ Consulting
- ☐ Training
- ☐ Packaging machines
- ☐ Blasting Publications
- ☐ Emulsion Pumps
- ☐ Blasting Mats
- ☐ Cross-linked Emulsion
- ☐ Emulsion Plants

- ☐ Computer Software, please specify:_____
- ☐ Blasting Machines, please specify:_____
- ☐ Emulsion Plants
- ☐ Seismographs, please specify:_____
- ☐ Dewatering Pumps, please specify:_____
- ☐ Blasting Workstation
- ☐ Remote Blasting Machines
- ☐ Emulsion Technology

Name:		
Company:		
Address:		
City:	State:	Zip Code:
Country:		
Phone:	Fax:	

Mail this coupon to Precision Blasting, P.O. Box 189, Montville, OH 44064 USA or fax to (440) 968-3967

Email: Info@idc-pbs.com Phone: (440)-474-6700